MAY '08

ED

COUNTRY EXPLORERS

VENEZUELA

Helga Jones

Lerner Publications Company • Minneapolis

Lerner Publications Company
A division of Lerner Publishing Group, Inc.
241 First Avenue North
Minneapolis, MN 55401 U.S.A.

Website address: www.lernerbooks.com

Library of Congress Cataloging-in-Publication Data

Jones, Helga.
 Venezuela / by Helga Jones.
  p. cm. — (Country explorers)
 Includes index.
  ISBN-13: 978-0-8225-8663-0 (lib. bdg. : alk. paper)
  1. Venezuela—Juvenile literature. 2. Venezuela—Geography—
 Juvenile literature. I. Title.
 F2308.5.J663 2008
 987—dc22   2007024892

Manufactured in the United States of America
1 2 3 4 5 6 – PA – 13 12 11 10 09 08

Table of Contents

Welcome!

Venezuela is easy to find on a world map. First, look for the continent of South America. Search the northern part of the continent for Venezuela. There it is—between Colombia and Guyana. Venezuela shares its southern border with Brazil. The waters of the Caribbean Sea and the Atlantic Ocean splash Venezuela's coast.

Venezuela's Angel Falls is the tallest waterfall in the world.

4

ATLANTIC
OCEAN

CARIBBEAN SEA

Caracas

MARGARITA
ISLAND

Maracaibo

LAKE
MARACAIBO

Valencia

ORINOCO
DELTA

LLANOS

VENEZUELA

LLANOS

ORINOCO RIVER

PICO BOLÍVAR

ARAUCA RIVER

GUYANA

ANGEL
FALLS

ANDES MTNS.

GUIANA HIGHLANDS

COLOMBIA

ORINOCO RIVER

MILES
0   50   100   150   200
0   50 100 150 200 250 300
KILOMETERS

rain forest
plains
highlands
lowlands
mountains
country's capital

BRAZIL

Peaks and Plains

Part of the Andes is in Venezuela. It is the biggest chain of mountains in South America. Mountain ranges spike the land along the border with Colombia and on the Venezuelan coast.

The northern city of Mérida lies in the Andes Mountains.

Southeast of the mountains, the land flattens out. Plains called the Llanos stretch across the middle of Venezuela. Hills roll through the Guiana Highlands. They cover most of the land south of the Llanos.

Map Whiz Quiz

Take a look at the map on page 5. Trace the outline of Venezuela onto a sheet of paper. Look for the Caribbean Sea. Mark this end of your map with an *N* for north. Find the country of Brazil. Mark this end of the map with an *S* for south. Can you spot Colombia? Mark this area with a *W* for west. How about Guyana? Mark this with an *E* for east. Look for the Orinoco River. Trace its path with a blue crayon.

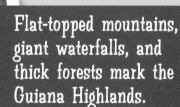

Flat-topped mountains, giant waterfalls, and thick forests mark the Guiana Highlands.

7

Big River

Big rivers cross the Llanos. The Orinoco is the largest. It flows through miles and miles of rain forest. The river empties into the Atlantic Ocean at the Orinoco Delta.

The sun sets over the water near the Orinoco Delta.

Thousands of birds and large rodents called capybaras come to the Llanos when the rivers flood.

Big River Animals

On a trip down the Orinoco River, you may see long-snouted river dolphins or manatees in the water. Crocodiles live on the banks of the river. Some crocodiles grow up to 20 feet (6 meters) long! Snakes called anacondas are even bigger. They chomp down crocs for lunch.

Venezuela's rivers change size with the seasons. In the summer, little rain falls. Small rivers dry up. Winter rains flood the rivers, forming big lagoons.

Watch out for Orinoco crocodiles!

This is a tapir.

Green All Over

Green rain forests thrive in southeastern Venezuela. The weather is hot and wet there. Some trees grow to be 150 feet (46 meters) tall. That's as tall as three telephone poles stacked on top of one another! Climbing vines wind up and around the tree trunks. Parrots, hummingbirds, and toucans fly through the treetops. Jaguars and tapirs roam the forest ground. Tapirs look like big pigs with pointy snouts.

Dear Mom and Dad,
Our trip to Venezuela has been really fun. Yesterday, we went with Grandpa to the island of Margarita. We took a boat ride through the manglares. They are tunnels made by small trees and bushes that grow in salty water. It was supercool! We also visited an old Spanish fort that overlooks the ocean. At the beach, we built our own fort out of sand.

¡Adiós!

Your Son

Your Tow

Anywhere

Venezuela

First People

The first people to live in Venezuela belonged to the Arawak, the Carib, and the Timoto-Cuica groups. Men hunted and fished. Women grew a root called cassava and gathered fruits such as plantains. Plantains look like long bananas.

This woman and her children are Warao Indians. They live in the Orinoco Delta.

12

The Yanomami people still live in the rain forests as their ancestors did. Many Yanomami families sleep in hammocks under a big roof made of palm leaves.

The Yanomami use the plants and animals of the rain forest.

From Spain

In 1498, European explorer Christopher Columbus landed in what would become Venezuela. Folks back in Spain heard stories of this rich land in South America. A few years later, groups of Spaniards moved to the continent to look for pearls and gold.

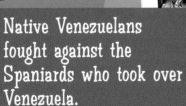

Native Venezuelans fought against the Spaniards who took over Venezuela.

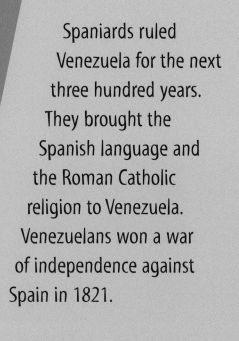

Spaniards ruled Venezuela for the next three hundred years. They brought the Spanish language and the Roman Catholic religion to Venezuela. Venezuelans won a war of independence against Spain in 1821.

Simón Bolívar is a hero in Venezuela. He led Venezuelans in their fight against Spain's control.

15

Who Is Venezuelan?

Most Venezuelans are Indian, European, or African. Many people are mestizos. That means that they have Spanish and Indian ancestors.

Venezuelan children pose for a picture.

16

Other Venezuelans are mulattoes. They are people of mixed African and European backgrounds. Long ago, slave traders brought people from Africa to Venezuela to work the land. Over time, the European settlers had children with the Africans. There are still many mulatto communities along the Caribbean Sea.

New Immigrants

People from other countries live in Venezuela too. They or their families came from places such as Italy, Portugal, Germany, or Colombia.

A Venezuelan man watches people pass by on the street.

City Living

Most Venezuelans live in cities. That's where they find jobs in factories, stores, hotels, or restaurants. The three biggest cities—Caracas, Maracaibo, and Valencia—are located in the north.

The city of Maracaibo lies on the shore of Lake Maracaibo. Oil was discovered in the lake in 1914.

Caracas is Venezuela's capital. It is a modern city filled with towering office buildings. Most people live in tall apartment buildings. But many poor people live in barrios. These neighborhoods of shacks are often built along a city's edges.

High-rise apartments are not far from barrio houses in Caracas.

These Venezuelan coffee beans are ready to be picked.

Country Life

Some Venezuelans live in the countryside—mostly in the Andes and in the Llanos. Many are farmers who grow coffee or cacao. Cacao is used to make chocolate.

This village is in Venezuela's Andes.

On the plains, cattle ranches and large farms called plantations are quite spread out. Cowboys called *llaneros* ride their horses across the plains to round up cattle.

A llanero watches over his cattle on the Llanos.

This crowded autopista leads to Caracas.

Get Going!

How does your family get around? In Venezuela, highways called *autopistas* connect the cities. Many autopistas run through Caracas. Folks zip from place to place in cars, buses, or taxis. The subway is known as El Metro. It speeds through the city in underground tunnels.

In the country, people use sturdy trucks to get around. When rain floods the roads, some people hop onto horses or donkeys. Others get around in boats.

In some parts of Venezuela, canoes are the best way to travel.

Family Time

Families are an important part of Venezuelan life. Many kids share a home with their parents, grandparents, and other relatives. Grandpa and Grandma watch young children while the parents are at work.

This large family lives in the northern city of Barquisimeto.

Venezuelan kids also have godparents. These people are usually good friends or relatives. Godparents buy kids gifts on birthdays and Christmas. As godchildren grow up, their godparents give them advice and help them through life.

All in the Family

Here are the Spanish words for family members. Practice them on your own family. See if they understand you!

grandfather	abuelo (ah-BWAY-loh)
grandmother	abuela (ah-BWAY-lah)
father	padre (PAH-dray)
mother	madre (MAH-dray)
uncle	tío (TEE-oh)
aunt	tía (TEE-ah)
son	hijo (EE-hoh)
daughter	hija (EE-hah)
brother	hermano (ehr-MAH-noh)
sister	hermana (ehr-MAH-nah)

Venezuelan women and children smile for the camera.

Time for School

All children between the ages of seven and fifteen must go to school. Elementary school is called *ciclo básico*. Students learn reading, writing, math, science, and social studies.

These kids attend a village school in north-western Venezuela.

School is five days a week from September to June. The first school bell rings at seven o'clock. Children bring a snack to eat during morning recess. At noon or one o'clock, students go home for lunch and to take a siesta (nap).

Many Venezuelan kids wear uniforms to school.

Say It in Spanish

Spanish is the official language of Venezuela. Venezuelans call it *castellano*. The Spanish alphabet has one more letter than the English alphabet. The extra letter is *ñ* (EHN-yay). It sounds like the *ny* in *canyon*.

The sign on this store in Caracas says that it is a supermarket.

Speaking Spanish

Here are a few Spanish phrases to try in Venezuela.

Hello!	¡Hola!	(OH-lah)
How are you?	¿Cómo estás?	(COH-moh ays-TAHS)
Very good.	Muy bien.	(MOOY BYEHN)
Awesome!	¡Chévere!	(CHAY-vay-ray)
Please.	Por favor.	(POHR fah-VOHR)
See you later!	¡Hasta luego!	(AHS-tah loo-AY-goh)
Thank you.	Gracias	(GRAH-see-ahs)
Good-bye!	¡Adiós!	(ah-dee-OHS)

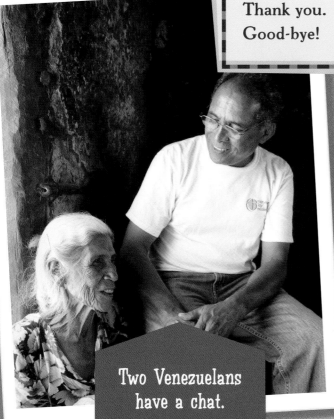

Two Venezuelans have a chat.

Ch (CHAY) and *ll* (EHL-yay) appear in many Spanish words. *Ll* sounds like the letter *y* in yellow. Two *r*s together—as in *perro* ("dog")—create a rolling *r*. In Spanish, a rolling *r* sounds a bit like a stick being dragged across a wooden fence.

29

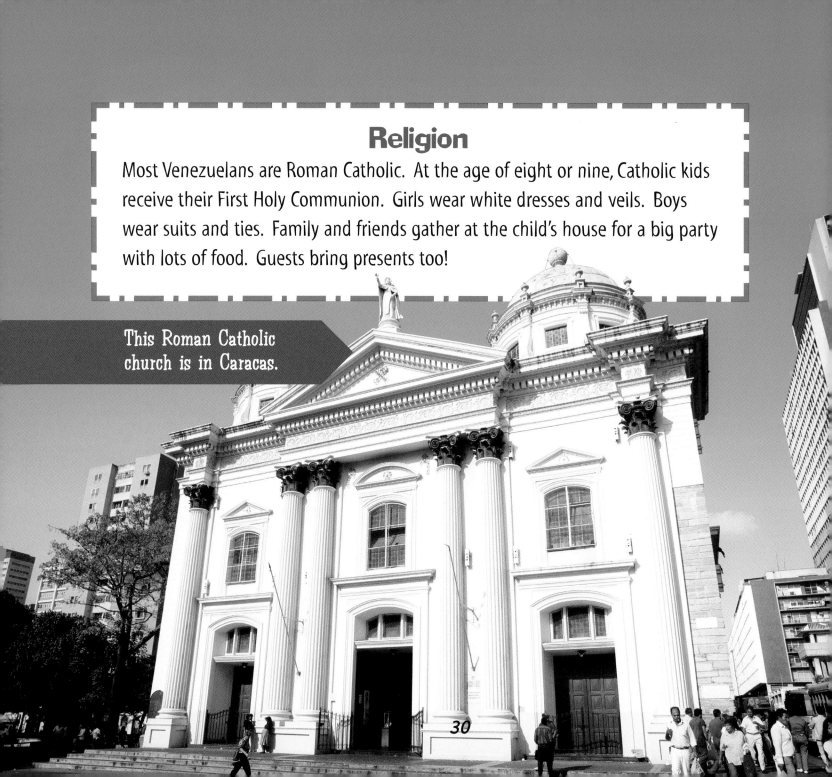

Religion

Most Venezuelans are Roman Catholic. At the age of eight or nine, Catholic kids receive their First Holy Communion. Girls wear white dresses and veils. Boys wear suits and ties. Family and friends gather at the child's house for a big party with lots of food. Guests bring presents too!

This Roman Catholic church is in Caracas.

30

Many villages across the country have a patron saint. Villagers believe the saint watches over and protects them. Each year, people honor the town's saint with a special church service, a parade, and a big dance.

The Lady of Coromoto is the patron saint of Venezuela.

Holidays

¡Feliz Navidad! That means "Merry Christmas" in Spanish. Venezuelan families get together for a party on Christmas Eve. At midnight, everyone goes to church. Venezuelans give each other gifts on Christmas Day.

A statue of baby Jesus is carried outside a church in Caracas on Christmas Day.

Palm Sunday and Easter are two other religious holidays. They are celebrated in the spring. On Palm Sunday, men race up hillsides to gather palm branches. They shout and shoot off firecrackers along the way.

A girl and her grandpa attend a church service in Caracas on Palm Sunday.

Clean Your Plate

Time to eat! Venezuelans love to cook on the barbecue. They grill beef from the Llanos and fresh fish from the Caribbean Sea. Plates are heaped with rice, a salad, and thick pieces of bread.

Seafood is popular with people on Venezuela's coast and islands.

34

To the Market

On Saturdays, many Venezuelans go to outdoor markets. There they can find fresh fruits and vegetables. Mangoes, oranges, and avocados are hot items.

If you would rather cook indoors, pabellón criollo is a tasty meal. It includes rice, black beans, fried plantains, and shredded beef.

Markets sell fruits and vegetables grown in Venezuela.

35

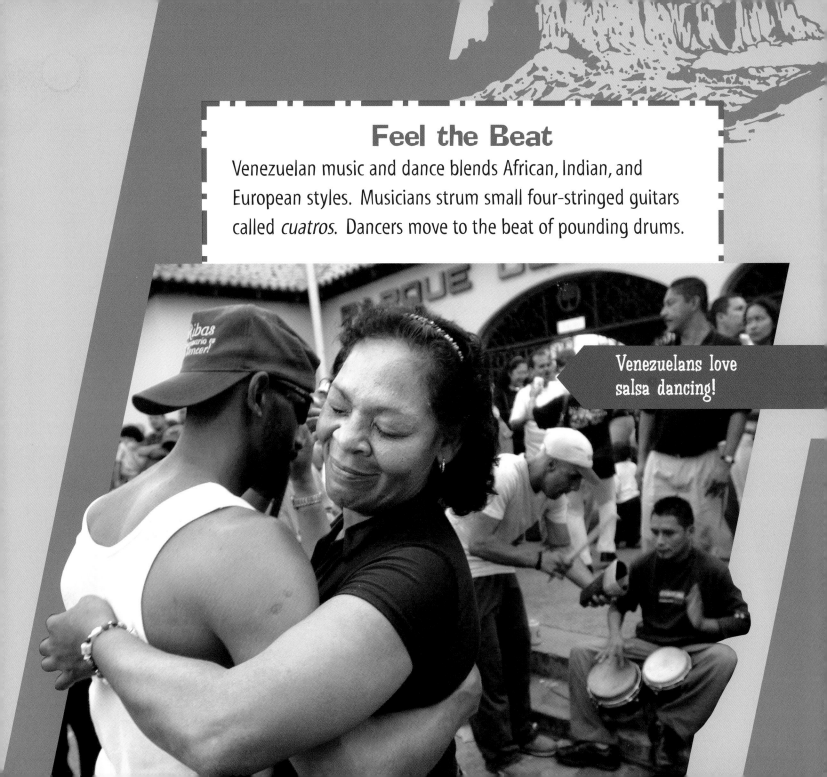

Feel the Beat

Venezuelan music and dance blends African, Indian, and European styles. Musicians strum small four-stringed guitars called *cuatros*. Dancers move to the beat of pounding drums.

Venezuelans love salsa dancing!

The song "Alma Llanera" (Soul of the Plains) is about the llaneros' friendship with the Arauca River. In the song "Carite," a big fish sings about how he likes to swim along the coast. But a fishing boat keeps following him. At the end of the song, the fisherman finally catches the fish.

Folk musicians play stringed instruments. The man in the center is playing the cuatro.

Listen to a Story

For many years, kids in Venezuela have snuggled up to their grandparents to listen to stories. Venezuelan folktales include Indian and Spanish stories. Many of the folktales try to explain why some animals look or act a certain way.

Folktales are passed down from grandparents to their children and grandchildren.

A colorful toucan sits in a tree.

A Venezuelan Folktale

Long ago, all birds in Venezuela were gray. One day, a cormorant bird caught a water snake in the river. The cormorant and some other birds killed the snake. All the birds admired the snake's colors.

"I wish my feathers were that colorful," the toucan said.

"Why don't you take some of the snake's colors?" the cormorant asked.

"Thanks, I think I will," the toucan replied. He picked blue for his eyes, yellow for his chest, and green, red, and yellow for his beak.

"You look beautiful," the hummingbirds said. "We want to be colorful too!" They flew over to the snake and picked a few colors. Other birds also chose colors before flying away.

Soon the cormorant was all alone. "There are no colors left for me," he said sadly. But when he looked again, he found some black and a few white spots for his back. And this is the story of how the birds got their colors.

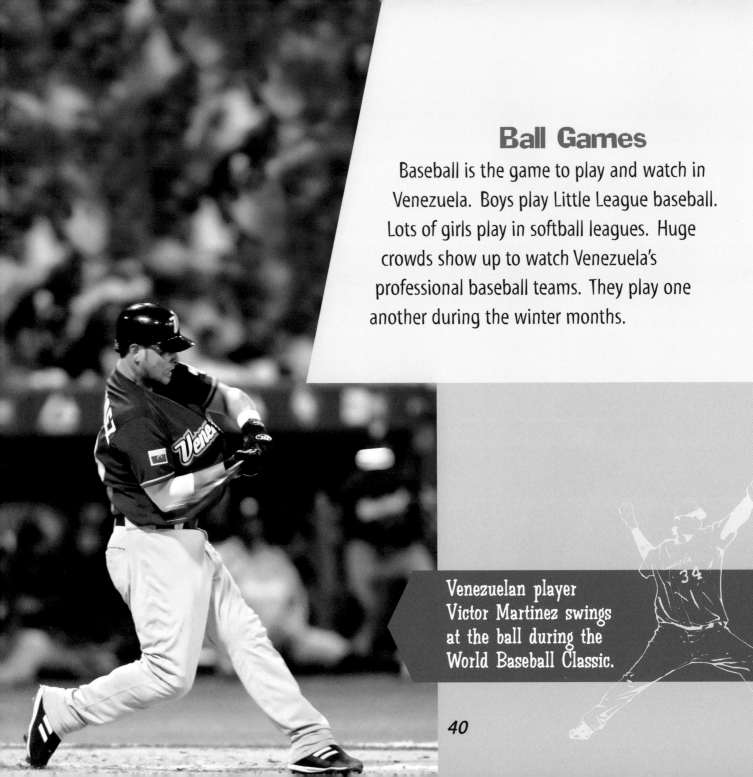

Ball Games

Baseball is the game to play and watch in Venezuela. Boys play Little League baseball. Lots of girls play in softball leagues. Huge crowds show up to watch Venezuela's professional baseball teams. They play one another during the winter months.

Venezuelan player Victor Martinez swings at the ball during the World Baseball Classic.

From March to July, the country follows basketball. Venezuela has eight professional teams.

Soccer is becoming more and more popular too. City teams play one another during the year. And Venezuela sends a team to compete in the World Cup. It's the biggest soccer championship in the world.

A Venezuelan basketball player tries to score.

A windsurfer cuts across the water near one of Venezuela's islands.

Fun after Hours

Venezuelans have plenty to do on weekends. Venezuela's nice weather allows folks to enjoy the outdoors all year. They can swim, surf, or fish in the sea. Other people hike or climb Venezuela's mountains. Families enjoy going to horse racetracks too.

Some folks would rather stay at home and watch TV. Venezuelan television shows are so popular that there are more homes with TV sets than with telephones! Even tiny tin shacks on hillsides have antennas on their roofs.

Many people tune in to news programs like this one. But Venezuelan soap operas are more fun to watch!

THE FLAG OF VENEZUELA

The flag of Venezuela has gone through many changes since 1806. That was the year Francisco de Miranda raised it as a symbol of Venezuela's fight for independence from Spain. Each star on the flag is for a province that was part of independent Venezuela. In 2006, the government added an eighth star. The flag's yellow stripe stands for Venezuela's wealth. The blue stripe is for the ocean. The red stripe stands for the blood of the men who fought for the country's independence. The symbol in the corner is Venezuela's coat of arms.

FAST FACTS

FULL COUNTRY NAME: República Bolivariana de Venezuela (Bolivarian Republic of Venezuela)

AREA: 352,144 square miles (912,050 square kilometers), or about the size of Texas and Oklahoma combined

MAIN LANDFORMS: the coast, the Andes mountain ranges, the Maracaibo lowlands, the Llanos (plains), the highlands called Guiana, the Amazon rain forest, the Orinoco Delta, Lake Maracaibo, the waterfall Angel Falls

MAJOR RIVERS: Orinoco, Caroní, Portuguesa, Arauca

ANIMALS AND THEIR HABITATS: red howler monkeys (rain forest); scarlet ibis (plains), jaguars, anteaters, tapirs, capybaras, turpials (plains and rain forest); Orinoco crocodiles, electric eels, manatees (rivers)

CAPITAL CITY: Caracas

OFFICIAL LANGUAGE: Spanish

POPULATION: about 27,500,000

GLOSSARY

ancestor: a relative, such as a great-great-great-grandparent, who lived long before you

barbecue: a way of cooking meat or fish over an open fire or over hot coals

barrio: the name for a city neighborhood in Spanish-speaking countries

coast: an area where the ocean or sea meets land

continent: any one of seven large areas of land. The continents are Africa, Antarctica, Asia, Australia, Europe, North America, and South America.

delta: an area where a river branches into many smaller rivers before flowing into a larger body of water

folktale: a timeless story told by word of mouth from grandparent to parent to child. Many folktales have been written down in books.

lagoon: a shallow pond that is often connected to a bigger body of water

mestizo: a person of mixed Spanish and Native American backgrounds

mountain range: a series, or group, of mountains

mulatto: a person of mixed black and white backgrounds

plain: a large area of flatland that is usually covered with grass and has few trees

rain forest: a thick, green forest that gets lots of rain each year

TO LEARN MORE

BOOKS

George, Jean Craighead. *One Day in the Tropical Rain Forest.* New York: Harper Trophy, 1995. A Venezuelan Indian boy and a scientist must save the rain forest while trying to capture a butterfly.

Manera, Alexandria. *Capybaras.* Chicago: Steadwell Books, 2003. This book describes the lives of these strange, giant rodents in the rain forests.

Mattern, Joanne. *Angel Falls: World's Highest Waterfall.* New York: PowerKids Press, 2002. Find out the facts about this beautiful waterfall in Venezuela.

Zuehlke, Jeffrey. *Johan Santana.* Minneapolis: Lerner Publications Company, 2007. Learn about the life and career of this baseball player and Cy Young Award winner from Venezuela.

WEBSITES

Embassy of Venezuela in the United States: Venezuela for Kids
http://www.embavenez-us.org/index
.php?pagina=kids.venezuela/intro.htm
Find facts on the history, people, places, culture, and symbols of Venezuela on this site.

Venezuela's Flag— EnchantedLearning.com
http://www.enchantedlearning.com/
southamerica/venezuela/flag
Visit this site for a history and printout of the Venezuelan flag and maps of the country.

INDEX

The images in this book are used with the permission of: © age fotostock/SuperStock, pp. 4, 9 (both), 10 (bottom), 11, 20 (left), 30; © Photofrenetic/Alamy, p. 6; © Jacques Jangoux/Peter Arnold, Inc., p. 7; © Woodfall Wild Images/Alamy, p. 8; © Jacques Jangoux/Visuals Unlimited, p. 10 (top); © Marion Kaplan/Alamy, p. 12; © Mark Edwards/Peter Arnold, Inc., p. 13; © The Print Collector/Alamy, p. 14; © Dave Saunders/Art Directors, p. 15; © Sean Sprague/Peter Arnold, Inc., pp. 16, 24, 25, 26, 29, 38; © Fredrik Naumann/Panos Picures, p. 17; © STR/AFP/Getty Images, p. 18; © Jacob Silberberg/Panos Pictures, pp. 19, 22, 28; © Mediacolor's/Alamy, p. 20 (right); © INTERFOTO Pressebildagentur/Alamy, p. 21; © Scott Kleinman/Stone/Getty Images, p. 23; © Martin Barlow/Art Directors, p. 27; © Pablo Corral V/CORBIS, p. 31; © Paula Bronstein/Getty Images, p. 32; AP Photo/Fernando Llano, p. 33; © Nicholas Pitt/Alamy, p. 34; © Travel Ink/Alamy, p. 35; AP Photo/Leslie Mazoch, pp. 36, 43; © Krzysztof Dydynski/Lonely Planet Images, p. 37; © Cagan Sekercioglu/Visuals Unlimited, p. 39; © Jimmy DeFlippo/USP/ZUMA Press, p. 40; © Wang Jiaowen/Color China Photos/ZUMA Press, p. 41; © Mike Schroeder/Peter Arnold, Inc., p. 42. Illustrations by © Bill Hauser/Independent Picture Service. Front cover: © Bob Gaspari/Alamy.